The Aztecs

Meredith Costain

Contents

The Aztec Civilization	3
The Huge City	4
Aztec Society	8
Clothing	12
Hairstyles	13
Food	14
Aztec Pictographs	16
Education	18
Aztec Gods	20
The Aztec Calendar	22
What Happened to the Aztecs?	23
Index	24

The Aztec Civilization

The Aztecs once ruled over much of the land that we now call Mexico. The center of their civilization was a huge city called Tenochtitlán, which the Aztecs built about 800 years ago.

Spanish explorers arrived in Mexico about 500 years ago and were amazed by Tenochtitlán. It was one of the biggest cities in the world at that time.

The ruins of Tenochtitlán can still be seen today.

The Huge City

Tenochtitlán was named after the Aztec leader, Tenoch. Tenoch believed that a god wanted him to build a city. He believed that he would know where to build the city when he saw an eagle on a cactus, eating a snake. Tenoch saw an eagle like this on an island in the middle of Lake Texcoco, so Tenochtitlán was built there. A picture of the eagle appears on the modern flag of Mexico.

The Aztecs were very clever builders. They built stone roads, called causeways, above the water to connect their island city to the mainland. They also used stone to build water channels to bring fresh water into the city.

In the early 1500s, there were around 60,000 buildings, and more than 250,000 people in Tenochtitlán.

This painting shows the city of Tenochtitlán.

Wealthy Aztecs lived in colorful two-story stone houses. The houses were built around a courtyard with a fountain and a garden filled with flowers. There were large rooms for eating, cooking, and sleeping.

The homes of commoners, or ordinary families, were much smaller and simpler. Most had only one room. The walls were made from mud bricks, or from grasses woven together and covered with mud. People sat and slept on mats on the floor. They kept their clothes in wooden boxes and cooked their food on open fires instead of stoves.

An Aztec family at home

The Aztecs built hundreds of temples for the gods they worshipped. Temples were usually built on top of pyramids. The Aztecs piled up huge mounds of earth to form the pyramids, then covered them with bricks made from mud or stone. They built steps up the sides, and at the very top, they built the temples.

Aztec Society

Many people in Aztec society worked on farms growing crops. It was very hard work, and everything had to be done by hand. There were no plows, carts, or farm animals to help.

Many people were also craft-workers and traders. Some made everyday items such as pots, baskets, mats, and cloth. Others used silver, gold, gemstones, and feathers to make beautiful jewelry and ornaments.

Aztec women worked in the home, cooking, weaving, and caring for their children.

Some Aztecs were nobles. Nobles were very wealthy, powerful, and important people in Aztec society. Priests and leaders of government were nobles. The Aztec ruler, or emperor, was chosen from a noble family.

Warriors

The Aztecs were fierce warriors. They fought with spears and clubs edged with blades. But Aztec warriors usually did not kill their enemies. They often captured them as prisoners.

The best warriors were called eagle warriors or jaguar warriors. Eagle fighters wore helmets decorated with eagle feathers. Jaguar fighters wore outfits made from jaguar skins.

It was a great honor to be a warrior, so most young boys wanted to be warriors when they grew up. All boys were trained at a young age to fight, whether they came from rich or poor families.

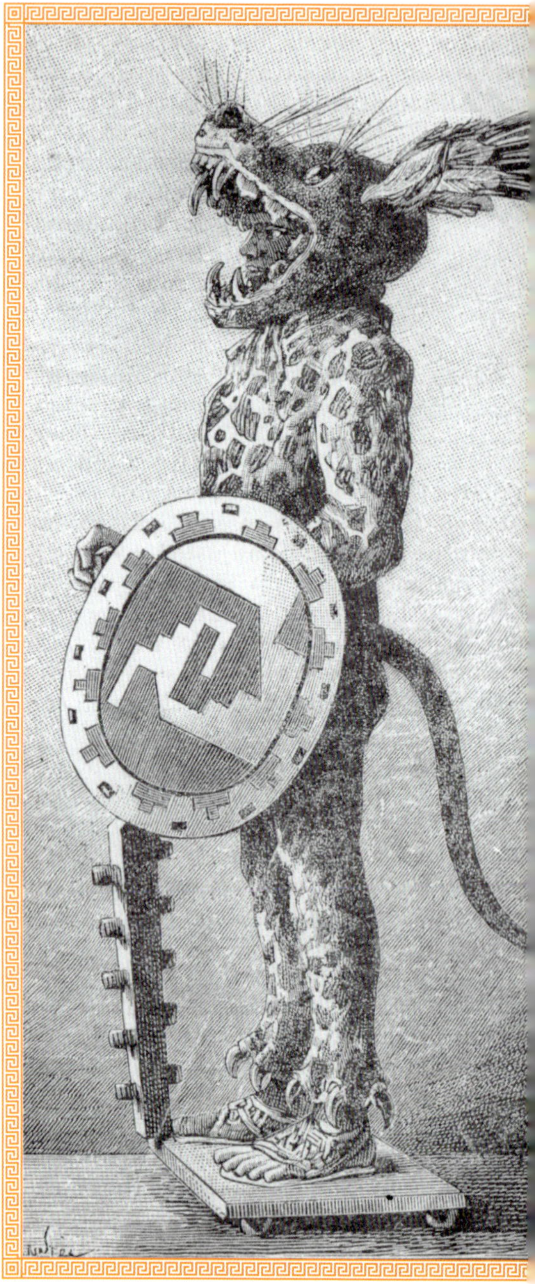

Sportsmen

The Aztecs played some games that required a lot of skill. During religious festivals, they sometimes played a fast-moving game called *tlachtli*. The game was played by two teams on a stone court. A ring made of stone was set high up on the wall of the court. To score, players had to flip a hard rubber ball through a stone ring. They were only allowed to touch the ball with their elbows, knees, or hips. Many players ended up with terrible bruises and injuries.

Clothing

In Aztec times, you could tell how important a person was by looking at his or her clothing.

Most Aztec men wore simple cloths wrapped around their waists, with another cloth knotted at the shoulder to form a cloak. Women wore long loose blouses and skirts that wrapped around their waists and covered their knees. The material for their clothing was made from plant fibers and was very rough and uncomfortable to wear.

However, people born into rich families wore brightly colored cloaks made from finely spun cotton. It was against the law for commoners or slaves to wear a cloak that came down below your knees! And only nobles were allowed to wear sandals on their feet.

Clothes worn by an Aztec ruler named Montezuma

Hairstyles

In Aztec times, you could tell a lot about a person by the way they wore their hair. Warriors knotted their hair on top of their heads.

You could tell if a woman was married by her hairstyle. A married woman wore her hair in braids, wound around her head. All other women and girls were allowed to wear their hair loose and flowing.

These women's hairstyles show whether or not they are married.

Food

The Aztecs grew many of the foods we eat today. They ate corn, avocados, and tomatoes. They made tortillas, tacos, and tamales.

One of the best things the Aztecs left to the world was chocolate! They crushed cacao beans with vanilla and spices and mixed them with water to make a frothy drink called *chocolatl*. In the Aztec culture, only warriors and nobles drank chocolate.

These Aztec farm workers are putting grain into storage jars.

The Aztecs in Tenochtitlán grew their crops on special fields called chinampas. They made the chinampas in marshy ground by building up earth and reeds.

Aztec Pictographs

The Aztecs were able to read and write. However, instead of using letters from an alphabet to form words, they used pictures. We call these pictographs.

Some pictographs showed one object or animal. The Aztecs used simple pictographs like this for the names of days. Here are the pictographs for four of their days.

water

rabbit

eagle

lizard

Scribes drew the outlines of the pictographs with pointed sticks and ink made from soot. Then they filled in the outlines with colors made from plants, shells, insects, and minerals. If they wanted to show that something was really important, they made that picture bigger than the others. Sometimes many pictographs were shown together.

Aztec pictographs

Education

Most Aztec children went to school. Boys from poor Aztec families went to free schools. They learned history, religion, music, dancing, and how to be good citizens. Most of their time, however, was spent doing hard work, such as digging ditches. This was to help them become tough and strong, so they could one day be good warriors. They were taught how to use weapons, and fought pretend battles with wooden sticks.

Boys from rich families went to school to learn how to read and write. They studied mathematics, poetry, and law. They were also taught how to become warriors. Once they left school, they would become priests, generals, judges, or government officials.

Girls from noble families were allowed to go to a school or temple where they trained to be healers. They spent much of their time there in silence or learning about religion and medicine.

When Aztec students learned about numbers and counting, they learned how to show numbers in pictographs.

The numbers from 1 to 19 were shown as dots or fingers.
20 was shown as a flag.
20 X 20 (400) was shown as a fir tree.
20 X 20 X 20 (8000) was shown as a pouch.

1

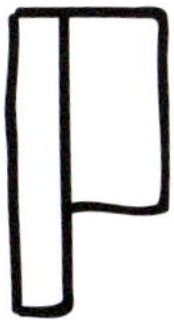

20

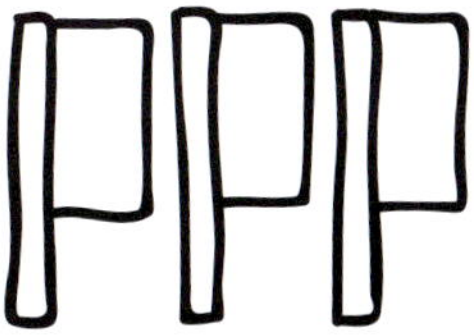

60

400

404

8000

Aztec Gods

The Aztecs believed that gods controlled everything that happened in their lives. They even controlled the weather and the crops that grew in the fields. The Aztecs believed it was very important to keep the gods happy.

The Aztecs worshipped hundreds of different gods. Tlaloc was the god of rain. Coatlicue was the goddess of earth and fire. Quetzalcoatl was the god of life. One of the most important gods was the war and sun god, Huitzilopochtli.

The Aztecs believed that unless they constantly prayed to the sun god, and gave him gifts every day, he would die. This would mean that the sun would not rise in the morning. Everything would be cold and dark, and nothing could grow or live.

All Aztecs celebrated at the many festivals and ceremonies held in honor of the gods. There was lots of singing and dancing to music played on drums, rattles, flutes, whistles, and trumpets made from shells.

Musicians at a festival to honor the gods

The Aztec Calendar

The Aztecs were very interested in the movement of the Earth and other planets around the sun. The Aztecs used this information to make a sun stone, which was their calendar. The sun stone divided the year into 365 days. There were 18 months, each containing 20 days. Every year there were five days left over called *nemontemi*. On these five days people would stop work and other normal activities and participate in festivals instead.

The Sun Stone was the Aztec calendar.

What Happened to the Aztecs?

In 1519, Spanish explorers landed in Mexico. When they saw the rich empire that the Aztecs had built, they decided to claim it for Spain. The Aztec warriors were soon defeated.

However, many of the Aztec ways and traditions still live on in Mexico. Some native people still speak the Aztec language and hold traditional religious ceremonies. They wear colorful hand-woven clothing and make delicate craftwork from silver, gold, and clay. And all over the world today people still eat chocolate!

An Aztec ceremony in modern-day Mexico

Index

calendar 22

clothing 12, 23

commoners 6, 12

education 18–19

farming 8, 14–15

food 14–15

gods 4, 7, 20–21

hairstyle 13

homes 6

nobles 9, 12, 14, 19

pyramids 7

temples 7, 19

Tenochtitlán 3–5

warriors 10, 13, 14, 18, 23